J. Y. Shantz

Narrative of a Journey to Manitoba

J. Y. Shantz

Narrative of a Journey to Manitoba

ISBN/EAN: 9783337127978

Printed in Europe, USA, Canada, Australia, Japan

Cover: Foto ©Andreas Hilbeck / pixelio.de

More available books at **www.hansebooks.com**

PROVINCE OF MANITOBA.

INFORMATION

FOR

TENDING EMIGRANTS,

PUBLISHED BY THE DEPARTMENT OF AGRICULTURE.

OTTAWA.

1874.

The information in this pamphlet is compiled, in as far as possible, from official sources.

Among the new matter it contains is a series of answers to questions from Mr. Kenneth Mackenzie, an Ontario farmer who has been settled for four years on the Assiniboine River. This information contains the record of the experience of a practical man.

The narrative of Mr. J. Y. Shantz, of Berlin, Ontario, is also inserted; together with a summary of the evidence taken before a Committee of the Senate, at Ottawa, in 1870; and other matter.

DEPARTMENT OF AGRICULTURE,
Ottawa, March, 1874

PROVINCE OF MANITOBA.

—◆●◆—

GENERAL FEATURES.

In the newly acquired North West Territory of Canada is the recently created Province of Manitoba. It contains about 9,000,000 acres of land; but it is comparatively a speck on the map of the vast Territory out of which it has been formed. The soil, which is mostly prairie, and covered with grass, is a deep alluvial deposit of unsurpassed richness. It produces bountiful crops of cereals, grasses, roots and vegetables. There is credible information, that, so rich and inexhaustible is the soil, wheat has been cropped off the same place for forty years without manure. It is especially a wheat growing soil, and is believed to contain the most favorable conditions for the growth of this grain on the continent. Strawberries, currants (red and black), raspberries, plums, cherries, blueberries, whortleberries, cranberries (both bush and marsh), grow wild and in abundance. Flax is very luxuriant. The wild grasses of the country, which are very nutritious, are particularly favorable for stock raising of all sorts. Cattle can be fattened in Manitoba, and driven to St. Paul without loss of weight. There are large tracts of woods along the streams. The beet root grows in great abundance, but the saccharine qualities of the sugar beet have not yet been tested.

Manitoba is situated in the middle of the continent, nearly equally distant between the Pole and the Equator and the Atlantic and Pacific Oceans. Its climate gives conditions of decided heat in summer and decided cold in winter. The snow goes away and ploughing begins in April, which is about the same time as in the older Provinces of Canada, and the Northern United States on the Atlantic Seaboard, and the North Western States of Minnesota and Wisconsin. The crops are harvested in August. The long sunny days of summer, bring vegetation of all sorts to rapid maturity. The days are warm and the nights cool. Autumn begins about the 20th September, when the regular frost sets in. The winter proper comprises the months of December, January, February and March. Spring comes in April. The summer months are part of May, June, July, August, and part of September. In winter the thermometer sinks to thirty and forty degrees below zero; but this degree of cold in the dry atmosphere of the North West does not produce any unpleasant sensations. The weather is not felt to be colder than that in the Province of Quebec, nor so cold as milder winters in climates where the frost, or even a less degree of cold than frost, is accompanied with dampness. The testimony is abundant, in fact universal, on this point.

Snow does not fall on the prairies to an average greater depth than eighteen inches, and buffaloes and horses graze out of doors all winter. They scratch the snow off the prairie grass on which they grow fat. Horned cattle graze out of doors part of the winter, but in some states of the weather they require to be brought in. Instances are, however, stated in which horned cattle graze out all winter.

Winnipeg, the capital of Manitoba, has not at present much more than the dimensions of a large village, but it is already beginning to receive an immigration, as well from the older Provinces of the Dominion as from the United States and Europe. It will probably, therefore, soon become a considerable town. Navigation is about to be opened between the Red River and the head waters of the Saskatchewan, above Fort Edmonton, near the base of the Rocky Mountains, by steamboat, a distance of over a thousand miles, as the crow flies, through prairie land of unsurpassed richness. The route to Manitoba from Thunder Bay to Fort Garry has been very greatly improved, and the Canadian Government conveys emigrants between these points for $10. The weight of luggage which emigrants can carry over this route is, however, limited to 450 lbs. each, and no package must exceed 150 lbs. weight, for convenience of transport over the portages.

It is intended to have steamers on the navigable waters of this route, during the coming season of navigation.

By the United States routes an emigrant may proceed by water to Duluth, and thence by the Northern Pacific Railway to Moorhead, a station on the Red River; whence there is steamboat navigation to Winnipeg.

There are other railway routes *via* St. Paul's, which afford facilities for travel to Manitoba.

A light buggy may be driven for a thousand miles in a straight line over the open prairie, which is adapted to the production of wheat, not only in the largest quantity to the acre, but of the best quality.

This tract of country to the east of the Rocky Mountains contains under the surface of its rich prairie land, one of the largest coal fields in the world, which in some places, crops out at the surface on the banks of the rivers. It is almost impossible to over-estimate the importance of this physical fact for the future of the Dominion. The rivers which run east from the Rocky Mountains are rich in gold deposits; and in fact mineral wealth of almost every kind is found in this territory.

The drawbacks of the country which have been found in the past are—1st. Want of markets; 2nd. Invasions of caterpillars; and 3rd, occasional untimely frosts. But the first of these drawbacks is beginning to disappear with the progress of settlement; the second is an evil which Manitoba suffers, in common with the Western United States, which are prosperous; and the third, with other parts of Canada and a great part of the continent of North America.

The accounts of settlers and travellers constitute information on which, at present, opinions may be formed of the Province of Manitoba. The most recent of these accounts is the statement of the experience of Mr. Kenneth Mackenzie, a farmer who emigrated from the Province of Ontario and settled on the Assiniboine River. A series of questions were sent to Mr. Mackenzie, to which he replied describing the country, the mode of farming and the results which he obtained. The information which he furnishes is put in a form to be understood by farmers, and will be found interesting to them :—

MR. KENNETH MACKENZIE'S STATEMENTS.

Question.—How long have you been a resident of Manitoba?

Answer.—Four years.

Q. From what part of Ontario or the old country did you come?

A. Scotland, in 1842, then twenty years of age ; lived in Puslinch, County of Wellington, twenty-five years.

Q. How many acres of land have you under cultivation at the present time?

A. One hundred and forty under crop, and about sixty more broken this summer. We plough the first breaking two inches deep, and the next spring or fall plough it a second time, and turn up two inches more.

Q. Is it broken from bush or prairie land ?

A. Prairie.

Q. What is the quality of the soil, and of what does it consist ?

A. Around Fort Garry to Poplar Point rather clayey with rich alluvial soil above ; from Poplar Point west, clay loam with fine alluvial soil above, but in several places sandy loam. There are to the south-west of here places too sandy for good farming land.

Q. Do you consider it good agricultural productive soil ?

A. I never saw better, except that which is too sandy. There are settlers north-west from here for fully thirty miles, and although newly settled, they have good, fair crops, and no grasshoppers.

Q. Is prairie hard to break ?

A When the summer is wet or moist I would sooner break it than old spear grass sod, as we do not require to break so deep.

Q. What months do you consider best to break it in ?

A. June and July, but earlier will do if you have time, as later does not answer so well.

Q. What kind of a plough do you use for breaking ?

A. American, made by John Deen Moline, but other Americans make good breaking ploughs—light with gauge wheel in front, and re olv ng coulter—mould boards and coulter and shear, all steel. No use for any other material here in ploughs but steel. The soil is rich and very adhesive, and even to steel it will stick a little in wet weather, more so after it is broken and cultivated.

Q. What kind, and whose make, of a plough do you consider best adapted both for breaking and after-ploughing ?

A. The American ploughs answer for both at present. I have a Canadian plough which does very well, but I think a good light Canadian, all steel, or even glass mould-board, would be better after the land begins to be old or long broken. We cannot go deep enough with the American ploughs when land is getting old and needy.

Q. How many horses or oxen do you use with each plough when breaking the prairie ?

A. On a twelve-inch breaker, we use one pair horses, or one yoke oxen. When sixteen-inch, we use three horses or two yoke oxen. I prefer twelve-nch ploughs to larger ones.

Q. How many acres will a good team break in a day ?

A. About one acre is a fair day's work, *i. e.,* day after day. Some, of course, will do more. The large plough and more teams will break one and a-half acres.

Q. How many ploughings do you give the land before cropping, and at what time ?

A. Two ploughings for first crop answers best, *i. e.* one light or 2 inch in summer, and then 2 inches more stirred up, next spring we plough both times same way, and not cross the first breaking. I have raised potatoes and turnips last year on first breaking, had a fafr crop, but would not like to depend on it if the season was dry.

Q. What crops do you grow most extensively ?

A. This year, spring wheat, 90 acres, barley, 30 acres, oats, 1 acre, peas, 8 acres, rye, 1 acre, flax, ¼ acre, potatoes, 6 acres; the rest, roots of various kinds, and clover and timothy.

Q. What kinds of fall wheat, if any, do you grow ?

A. I have tried fall wheat, but do not consider it a profitable crop to raise here at present.

Q. What kinds of spring wheat do you grow ?

A. Golden drop, Glasgow or Fife, and a little Rio Grand, I think it is called.

Q. How many bushels do you sow per acre ?

A. About 2 bushels per acre.

Q. What is the average yield per acre, one year with the other?

A. Fully 30 bushels ; I have had over 40.

Q. Does Indian corn grow well, and yield a good crop ?

A. It does not mature very well. They have a small kind that ripens but I do not like it.

Q. What kind of barley do you grow ?

A. Common 4 rowed, but think any variety will do well.

Q. How many bushels do you grow per acre ?

A. About 2 bushels.

Q. What is the average yield per acre ?

A. About 35 bushels, but I have seen over 50 per acre.

Q. What kind of peas do you grow ?

A. Russian blue and small white peas.

Q. How many bushels do you sow per acre ?

A. A little over 2

Q. What is the average yield ?

A. I think this year about 20 or 25 per acre ; my land being new till this year, they did not do so well.

Q. What kind of oats do you grow ?

A. Black oats.

Q. How many bushels do you sow per acre ?

A. Two bushels.

Q. What is the average yield of bushels ?

A. I have but little, but I see fields from here to Poplar Point, I think will yield from 45 to 60 per acre.

Q. Do timothy and clover grow successfully ?

A. I have had both do well; but timothy seems to do best.

Q. Do rye and flax grow successfully ?

A. Rye is a fair crop, and flax I never saw better.

Q. How are the soil and climate suited to growing root crops ?

A. All kinds of roots and vegetables that I have raised each year have done very well.

Q. Are these crops troubled with flies and insects as in Ontario ?

A. I have heard some complain of grubs, but have not suffered any by them on my crops, and I have sown turnips in May and they did well, and all through June, and no flies to hurt.

Q. Has your settlement been troubled by the grasshoppers ?

A Not since I have been here. I am eight miles west of Portage la Prairie, and no settler was before me west of the Portage. Poplar Point is about 25 miles east of here, or 17 from Portugal.

Q. How many times have the crops been destroyed or injured by them ; at what season do their ravages generally commence ; and how long do they generally continue ?

A. In 1868 they destroyed all from Portage at that time to Fort Garry, and all settled. This year they destroyed all down on Red River or around Fort Garry, and partially up the Assiniboine River, up to Poplar Point, but no farther. There are several fair crops in Headingly and White Horse Plains, i. e. half way between P. Point and Fort Garry.

Q. Do you think that this plague will continue when the country is better settled and more land cultivated ?

A. I cannot positively say, but think their ravages are partial. Some may suffer, while others escape. They have only made three clear sweeps, I I am told since 1812, when the country was first settled, and then all the portion that was settled was a small spot round Fort Garry. Rev. Mr. Nesbitt had a good crop in Prince Albert mission, Saskatchewan in 1868.

Q. Are there any crops that they do not destroy ?

A. They are not so bad on peas as on other crops.

Q.—Are the grasshoppers the only plague that you have been subjected to since settling in the Province ?

Q.—I have not suffered any as yet from grasshoppers. Black birds were very bad at first, especially on oats, and that is the reason I had not more sown this year. I have not seen one-fifth so many this year as before. I intend, if spared, to sow more oats in future.

Q.—How do the seasons correspond with ours in Ontario?

A.—Fall and Spring are drier. About the middle of April Spring commences generally; but I sowed wheat this year on the 3rd of April, and ploughed in 1870 on the 5th of April.

Q.—Is the snow melted by the sun, wind or rain ?

A.—Nearly all goes with the sun.

Q.—Have you much rain during the Spring?

A.—Very little till May, June and July.

Q.—What time does the frost leave the ground ?

A.—About the 20th of April; in places it may be longer.

Q.—Have you much frost after growth commences ?

A.—I have seen a little in May, but I have not had any of my crops injured by frost since I came to Manitoba.

Q.—How soon may ploughing and sowing be done ?

A.—You may sow as soon as the ground is black or snow off. The frost was not three inches out when I sowed my first wheat; I have it now stacked and a good crop.

Q. Is the summer different from ours in Ontario ?

A. Generally rather drier and vegetation more rapid.

Q. Have you showers during May, June and July, and have you heavy dews at night ?

A. Yes.

Q. Is growth as rapid as in Ontario ?

A. I think more so.

Q. Have you any summer frosts ?

A. None whatever since I have been here to injure crops.

Q. When do you generally cut your hay ?

A. From 15th July to 15th September.

Q. Does wheat, barley, and oat harvest commence later or earlier than n Ontario ?

A. Later ; generally about first week in August.

Q. Is the Fall early wet or dry ?

A. Early ; generally dry.

Q. What date do frosts generally commence ?

A. First of the season about 8th or 10th September, but fine weather after.

Q. When does the winter commence ; how soon is the ground frozen and snow fall ?

A. Generally frozen about 10th or 12th November; snow about 1st December. Some seasons are earlier ; others later.

Q. Have you deep snow early in or during the winter ?

A. First three winters snow would average from 16 to 20 inches; last winter 10 inches. The frost is generally a steady freeze.

Q. Have you many severe drifting snow storms ?

A. Not any more than in Ontario, generally ; last season none, but that is an exception.

Q. Have you wood convenient, and what kind ?

A, From two to three miles ; greater part poplar, but some oak and white ash, and small ash leaf maple.

Q. How do you fence your fields ; with rails, wire, or sods ?

A. With rails.

Q. How deep do you have to dig to get water in yours as well as your neighboring settlements ? Is it good ?

A. Generally they get water from nine to eighteen feet, but in this locality it is not so easily got. We expect to have a test well this fall. Water, in some instances, tastes a little salty. We use creek water.

Q. Have you a hay meadow convenient ?

A. About two miles off I have a large one of my own.

Q. What grass grown in Ontario does prairie grass cut for hay most resemble ?

A. Beaver meadow hay; only ours here, I think, better, and more variety.

Q. Does it make good hay, and do cattle and horses feed well on it ?

A. It makes good hay for cattle, and they feed well on it, but I do not think it near so good for horses as timothy hay.

Q. What is the average yield in tons to the acre ?

A. From one ton to two and-a-half tons, different seasons and different g.asses vary a good deal.

Q. To what height does grass on the open prairie generally grow ?

A. On hard, dry prairies not over ten inches, but on hay meadows I have seen four feet.

Q. Is it as pasture equal to our timothy and clover in Ontario ?

A. No, it is much thinner, and does not start so readily as clover, when eaten or cropped.

Q. Do the grasshoppers at any time destroy this grass, or can it at all times be relied upon as pasture ?

A. They do a little cropping when very bad, but not to my knowledge to destroy it for hay or feed.

Q. How often do the settlers fire the prairie, and are your crops ever endangered by such fires ?

A. There is a law against setting out prairie fires. I have not suffered any by them: I plough a few furrows around my fields and fences.

Q. Is it necessary to burn the grass on the prairie every fall in order to have a good growth the following year ?

A. Not at all.

Q. Have you tried any fruit trees, if so, how have they done ?

A. I have a few apple trees from seed, not well attended to three years old. I do not think it very good for apples or pears, unless we have a very hardy kind ; Siberian will do well. Plums are very good, and likewise wild grapes, though small, grow finely on the banks of our streams, and better hops I never saw than grow here wild. We use them for our bread rising. Currants, raspberries and strawberries grow wild quite abundantly. I think the growth of apple trees too rapid, and wood does not ripen, the soil being rather rich and not much shelter in general.

Q. What kind of lumber is most plentiful, and what is the average price for good lumber ?

A. Poplar lumber heretofore, and from $25 to $30 per thousand ; now good fair pine is to be had at Fort Garry, dressed, for same price, and soon we will have a mill to cut up white wood pine, or rather spruce pine.

14

Q. Would you advise persons coming on from Ontario to settle as farmers, to bring stock, such as working horses, oxen, cows, sheep, pigs &c., or would you advise them to bring with them any machinery, such as reapers and mowers, waggons, ploughs, fanning mills, &c., or can they be bought as cheap in Manitoba as they are brought, when we count the heavy freights and risk in doing so?

A. I would not advise to bring many horses. At first they do not thrive so well. Besides grain is expensive till raised. Oxen I prefer at first. They do more work on rough feed, and are far less risky. I think nearly twenty per cent. of the horses die, or are useless the first two years after being here. If a farmer wants a driving mare or to breed, all well, but by far too many horses are brought in, till we have more timothy hay and oats raised. Oxen and cows thrive well, and none can go wrong to bring them in. They can be got here. Freight by United States route is very high. On immigrants' goods it costs in general about $5.50 per cwt. That is, counting bonding, &c. If got by Dawson route, I expect it will be considerably cheaper.

Q. What is the price of a good span of horses in Manitoba?

A. I think about fifteen to twenty per cent. higher than same quality in Ontario, no regular price; same for oxen, &c.

Q. What is the price of a good yoke of oxen?

A. I have sold them from $125, $130, $35, $40, $50, $65, $70, $85, to $200 and $210, the latter were prime, *i. e.*, here or in Ontario.

Q. What is the price of a good cow?

A. I sold them from $30 to $60.

Q What is the price of good sheep?

A. I have none; they would do well if people had pasture fenced; I think they would sell pretty high, but wool, as yet, has been cheap.

Q. What is the price of good pigs?

A. Probably about 20 per cent. over same quality in Ontario. There are some very good pigs here.

Q. What is the price of a combined reaper and mower?

A. From $200 to $240.

Q. What is the price of a good plough, also fanning mill?

A. Wooden ploughs Canadian, do. American, about $40. Fanning mill from $15 to $50, both far too high for all the work on them.

Q. Would it not be a good speculation to bring out some thorough bred stock, such as cattle, sheep, and pigs?

A. I think so. My thorough-bred cattle thrive well here both summer and winter.

Q. How do you think the country is situated for dairy, cheese, and butter making?

A. Very well, just the thing required.

Q, Have you always a ready market for your produce?

A. Can sell nearly all I raise at the door.

Q. What is the average price?

A. Wheat, I sold last season about 1,000 bushels for $1.50; two seasons before it was about $1.25. Barley, from 75 cents to $1·12½; oats, from 75 cents to $1; peas, from $1 to $1.25; potatoes, from 62½ cents to 87½ cents; butter, from 25 cents to 37½ cents per lb.; eggs, from 20 cents to 25 cents per dozen; cheese, from 25 cents to 30 cents per lb.

Q. What season of the year would you advise settlers (with or without families, who intend to settle as farmers) to come in?

A. In spring if possible; but any season will do. I would advise immigrants with families to rent the first year or "share," and take a little time to select their location, and then to work and put in a crop, on the place they rent; generally plenty of farms can be got to rent or share. My reason for not raising more oats is, that the blackbirds heretofore were very troublesome, and seemed worse on the oats, but there is not now the one-fifth quantity of them that there used to be, and I hear they are generally worst at first. I intend to sow fully 20 acres next year (I would sow more if it were ready), with carrots, turnips, and mangold wurzel. These crops grow well, but the want of root houses is a disadvantage at present. I have a gang plough, but have scarcely used it yet, as I have been delayed breaking ground by taking in stock from the States. Last year I imported 84 cattle, and this year over 200, from the increase of which I now have fully 300 head. I am selling some daily, and purpose disposing of all the surplus I do not intend to winter, by auction, on the day after our County Exhibition, 2nd October. I am desirous of seeing good stock scattered through the Province as soon as possible. All my cows are served with thoroughbred Durham Bulls, and I have 3 thoroughbred calves, and one aged bull. Last season I sold at fair prices one thoroughbred bull and one calf. The country west or rather north west is better watered and wooded, and of better soil than that south and south west. All the land around here, say from 30 miles west, *i. e.,* third crossing of White Mud or Palestine River, to say 25 miles east, or Poplar Point is rapidly filling up, especially this summer, but plenty is

to be had all the way westward to the Rocky Mountains. I think few countries
in the world are superior to ours for agricultural purposes, and although the
winter is hard and long, cattle if provided for, thrive well. I wintered 91 head
last winter, and lost none, all turning out well in the spring. Most of them had
only rough open sheds for shelter, and ran loose. We have none of the wet
sleet in spring and fall that hurts cattle elsewhere. We are now stacking our
grain, and I think my average will be fully 36 bushels per acre all round; last
year I had 32 bushels per acre. I raised about 300 bushels of onions last year,
and sold them readily at $2 per bushel, and I expect fully as good a crop this
year, with the same, if not a better price, as but few are raised round Fort
Garry. Such prices, however, cannot last long, but as implements, &c., get
cheaper, we can afford to sell for less.

I again say, bring fewer horses into the country, but as much other stock
and implements as possible. First-class marsh harvesters, or machines which
will employ two men binding, and of the most improved make, are wanted.
I have two combined ones made by Sanger & Co., Hamilton. which answer
well, but those that will cut wider and quicker are required. There are no hills,
stumps, or stones here to trouble us, and I have not a single rood lodged this
year, although my crops are very heavy. Straw is generally stiff here, and not
apt to lodge. This year we have excellent crops of potatoes, and a neighbour
of mine, Mr. Hugh Grant, yesterday, dug an early rose potato weighing over
two pounds, and not then full grown. I think grain drills or broad-cast sowers
would be an improvement, as it is generally windy here in Spring. They
should be wider than those used in Ontario, say from eleven to twelve feet.
Instead of importing more cattle next year, I purpose breaking up more land,
as there will be a duty after 12th May next of 15 per cent. on American cattle,
instead of the 4 per cent. now paid. Large numbers have been brought in this
year, which will help to stock the country, as native cattle do well to cross with
improved breeds. Thorough-breds stand the winter equally as well as native
stock. 1 never saw better buckwheat in Ontario than the few patches grown
here. I think by ploughing round our farms, and planting lines of trees, we
could have shelter, and live posts to which wire fences could be attached with
small staples. Timber grows fast here. If we had yellow or golden willow,
which grows rapidly from cuttings, it would do well. Poles that I planted of
black poplar or balm of gilead are shooting out, and we could plant hardier and
better trees amongst them, which, though slower of growth, would replace
them. In several localities the Indians make maple sugar from small trees

and if some enterprising person or company would begin the manufacture of salt on Lake Manitoba, or to the north west of it, it would be a profitable business, and confer a benefit on the country as it is very dear. The half-breeds manufacture it, but on a very small scale, and it is of poor quality, being made in rusty kettles. I am told the brine is nearly as strong as at Goderich, and the deepest well was only fourteen feet. Timber is found within a mile of the brine springs, and whitefish is abundant where the little Saskatchewan empties into the lake at Fairford. Salt, rusty as it is, has sold here at from $2 to $3 per bushel of 60 lbs. If it were more reasonable it would be a great improvement to our hay, which cattle would devour more eagerly.

Waggons are generally heavily built, and so are the ploughs. When our makers take pattern from American machines, their work is cheaper. If we had a through route of our own, Canadian made machines would be cheaper, as in the present bonding system through the States, the Americans endeavour to take every advantage of the Immigrant, by misrepresentations and otherwise. I saw a great deal of that work when I was with the Menonite deputation, an American sticking to them even after they were here, and making all sorts of false representations. As however the Menonites are a shrewd people, they will weigh matters carefully before believing everything they hear. With all the flattering inducements held out, I have not seen grain or other crops in either Minnesota or Dakotah to equal ours in Manitoba. I have been in these States in all seasons of the year, and have friends farming in Minnesota, who are desirous if they can sell out of coming here. Whilst I was there, wheat was selling for 70 cents (greenbacks), and oats for 18 cents per bushel. Cattle and horses are fully as cheap if not cheaper than in Ontario ; their taxes are enormous, but yet we have had no taxes here. I, however, have never advised any one to come here, either from Ontario or the States, lest they should be dissatisfied and grumble, as some do wherever they go. Let every one come and judge for himself. I have seen people newly arrived from the old country, grumble for a time, and afterwards you could not induce them to go back. Some that did go back soon returned. I have heard of some faint-hearted Canadians, who frightened with tales of grasshoppers and other drawbacks, returned without even examining the country, but I think we are well rid of such a class. We have a large increase this year, principally from Canada, and I think they are likely to prove good settlers. I think, however, immigrants from the old country will be better off, as the population there is denser with less chances, whilst Ontario for those who are already settled, there offers as good a chance as here, without their moving. I have never seen better barns and out-buildings, better farming, or more permanent improvements than Ontario possesses. Of course we are backward in these things as yet, but we use machinery of the most improved kind for getting in our first crops, and buildings, with other requisites, will soon follow, if our country keeps on prospering, of which there is little doubt, if we only get through communication established on our own soil. We have plenty of coal, iron, lead, silver, copper, pitch, tar, salt, and various other materials. The country is for the most part level, and easy for the construction of railroads. The grasshoppers that came here, are driven by the wind from the deserts south of us. Our storms are not so bad as those in Minnesota, as the reports of the last few winters shew. Immigrants should all bring seed grain with them, as change benefits grain, and I may here mention as an instance of the adaptability of this country for wheat raising, that a variety called the "English wheat," brought from England where it had been grown with the same soil for 30 years, yields well here.

I assure you I have not in any instance overdrawn my statements, as I would rather it should be found I had under-estimated than exaggerated. Of course some seasons may differ from what I have seen, but if there are none worse than what I have experienced there is no room for complaint. The luxuries that are enjoyed in Ontario of course we cannot look for here. Even in the matter of fruit, if apples and pears fail to succeed here, railway communication if we had it, would bring them from Ontario or British Columbia. Perseverance in cultivation may yet give us a supply of fruit, though it is a matter of uncertainty whether it can be raised here, especially the finer kinds.

STATEMENTS MADE BEFORE A COMMITTEE OF THE SENATE.

Evidence of a similar character to that of Mr. Kenneth Mackenzie was taken before a Committee of the Senate of Canada, during the session of 1870, that House taking advantage of the presence of a number of persons from Manitoba, at that time in Ottawa, to make enquiries from them respecting the farming capabilities of that Province.

The following is a summary of the answers given to the Committee. It will be seen that they agree in the main with the statements of Mr. Kenneth Mackenzie.

MR. JOHN JAMES SETTER'S EVIDENCE.

The first witness examined was Mr. John James Setter, a school teacher and farmer who lives at Portage Laprairie. He was born at Red River, and had resided there all his life, except three years, 1856-7-8 he spent in the State of Minnesota. He had travelled about 110 miles west, on the Assiniboine, in the territory. Between that river and the boundary line, the country is divided between woods and prairie. The woods are always found on the banks of streams. Trees consist of oak, ash, elm and poplar for the most part; there are also pine and cedar. The alluvial deposit varies in depth. At Red River it is about a foot deep; whilst on the Assinniboine, in the neighbourhood of the Portage, it is three feet in depth, and in some places six. White mud underlies the alluvial deposit in the Portage section, and clay in the Red River. The wild grass on witness's farm is the ordinary prairie grass. It grows in the bottoms so tall that you can tie it over a horses back in walking through it, but the ordinary grass is short. He raises wheat; this weighs 64 lbs. to a bushel, but he has seen it weigh 68 lbs. Barley, oats, peas, potatoes, turnips and carrots are also raised. A variety of Indian Corn is used, and might be generally, but the people don't care about it. They generally put crops in from the middle of April to the middle of May, and harvest in August. They have never had the potato disease nor the weevil in wheat. Witness did not think there were any farms on the wooded lands; but the soil in the woods seems to be richer than on the prairie. Coal has been discovered 40 miles from Portage La Prairie, by Indians, cropping out on the river banks. They have frosts in September, but not sufficient to blanch the prairie grass. There is a kind of grass which remains green at the bottom all winter. Horned cattle are kept in, in winter; but horses may run out all winter. They feed cattle in the winter. One year he bought a new place, and being short of stabling he left out some of his cattle, and these were the fattest in the spring. They were only sheltered from winds, Snow is generally a foot and a half deep; but in places there are drifts. Weather in winter is dry, and there are no sleety storms. Temperature at times 43° and 44° below zero, but very rarely. Some of his neighbours have left 30 or 40 horses running at large all winter for about ten years. They live on prairie grass. When he was in Minnesota it was 41° below zero. They can move about in the cold weather with comfort. They have no thaws in winter, Snow begins about middle or latter part of November. Winter is steady. Spring commences at end of March and first of April. The roads are sufficient for carriages and all the smaller streams are bridged. From his place to Fort Garry there is a good road, Average height of the prairie grass is not more than a foot. The principal farmers are English and Scotch. There are some rabbits, and the birds are ducks, geese, cranes, swans, snipe, a small partridge, prairie chickens and pigeons. The heat at midsummer goes as high as 90°. Warm weather commences at middle of May. Nights are generally cool. Oats do well. Potatoes do well, as do also carrots and turnips. Witness said he had not eaten a good potato since he came to Canada. The grasshoppers did not make their appearance till 1857, but had heard they had been in the early days of the settlement. There is a saw mill at Lake Winnipeg. Of fish, they have white fish, sturgeon of a large size—from 100 to 200 lbs.—cat fish, perch, pike and gold eyes. Population of Portage La Prairie is about 300. "Natives, some Canadians, but no French." They have three Episcopalian churches. Presbyterians have their services in a private house at present. The settlement is entirely Protestant. There is a high school belonging to the Protestants, Bishop Macrae's, at St. John's, where they teach classics, mathematics and theology. There are no Protestants at St. Boniface. There is a splendid stone cathedral belonging to the Catholics. He considered Red River a finer country than the State of Minnesota. "It is the best country I have ever seen." The only thing to detract from its agricultural advantages is, that is so far from the sea board.

MR. JOSEPH MONKMAN'S EVIDENCE.

Joseph Monkman (half-breed, examined.—He lives in St. Peter's Parish, Indian Settlement. Speaks English, Chippewa and Cree. His father was an Englishman, and his mother a native of the Cree tribe. He has been as far north as the Norway House, at the extremity of Lake Winnipeg. He has also been up the Saskatchewan River, as far as Moose Lake, and as far as Carlton House, on the North Branch of the Saskatchewan. He has visited the Touchwood Hills, and been along the Qu' Appelle River. Knows the neighbourhood of Rainy Lake and the Lake of the Woods. He had heard Mr. Setter's observations about the capabilities of the country. He agreed in them. Mr. Setter has not overrated the advantages of the country. There are pines of three feet diameter. Red River is navigated as far as Fort Abercrombie, 290 miles from American territory. Witness farms himself. Last year he had a crop of wheat so heavy that it could not support itself. He sowed his wheat on 22nd April. One bushel sown yields 35. He has seen one grain of wheat make 55 heads. About 65 or 66 lbs. is the average. Barley exceeds wheat in luxuriance. He has seen a crop come off the same land for 25 years—the last much about the same as the first. It is very uncommon for the late frosts to injure grain. He has had none injured where he lives. Potatoes are invariably fine. He has grown them 2 lbs. each. He keeps 30 or 50 cattle and horses there, and houses his horses, but they can winter out. Snow is considered deep at three feet. Hemp grows taller than himself. They make maple sugar. There are a good many American merchants about Fort Garry. Water can be got anywhere they dig on the plains. Fifty miles along the shore of Manitoba Lake as good crops have been raised as on the banks of Red River. He had seen fine wheat 250 miles north of Red River. Passing Fort Pelly, the country is full of lakes and brackish water. It is a capital place for cattle. He does not think the frost in the country is at all an injury to farming. He manures his farm very little. He has seen a pumpkin that weighed 23 lbs; They have melons of all kinds.

REV. W. FLETCHER'S EVIDENCE.

The *Rev. William Fletcher*, examined, stated—Was born in Aberdeenshire, Scotland, and went to Portage La Prairie in 1868, from Carlisle, Ontario. Had previously been in Canada over 20 years, and is a minister of the Canada Presbyterian Church. He has been over a great deal of the Red River country from Portage down the Assinniboine to Fort Garry, and from Fort Garry to Stone Fort on Red River. There are 150 Presbyterian families in this district. From Lake Winnipeg to Fort Garry the people are almost entirely Protestant, on both sides of the river. The Protestant Churches mix a great deal. There are 10 or 12 of the Church of England, 4 of Presbyterians, and 3 other places of meeting in private houses ; 5 or 6 Wesleyan Methodist places of meeting. He believed the Catholics and Protestants in the settlement were about equal in numbers. Many of the Catholic Churches are built at considerable cost, of stone. He should think the cold averaged 30° below zero' The range is more equal than in Canada. He has known it as cold as 40° below zero. On the Assinniboine, seed time began last year on April 16th, and cattle fed then on the wild grass just outside the fences. The wild grass seemed to be refreshed with the winter's snow, and cattle ate it greedily. They prefer it to hay. They had not ploughed before the 16th of April, and then there was some frost in the ground. There has been no potato disease. He has seen as excellent vegetables as he ever saw in Canada. On an acre of cabbage not a head wanting, and each ten inches. Indian corn might not be a safe crop, but some early varieties would ripen. Wheat is harvested fully as early as in Canada West. Usual time of harvest is August. He would say the yield of wheat was 30 to 35 bushels per acre. His opinion was that all the cereals did not give less than 20 returns to the bushel down. Grasshoppers were again feared. The weevil and midge are not in the country. He has seen heads of grain growing 5 inches long without a single grain missing. The club wheat he has seen growing is longer than any he has seen in Canada. As compared with Canada as a home for immigrants there are some things which cannot be procured, but the country is favorable for farming, and a living can be got at far less cost of labor. The prairie grass returns where the sod has been broken by the plough. The land is very easily drained.

MR. DONALD CODD'S EVIDENCE.

Mr. Donald Codd.—Is a draughtsman. Was born in England. Resides in Ottawa. Went to Red River in June, 1869. Country between Oak Point and Fort Garry is excellent land. It is all Prairie with clumps of trees, small oak and poplar chiefly. He found the winters very much like the winters at Ottawa, only there were no decided thaws. In summer he remembers the thermometer 92° and 93° in the shade in August, and that was considered a hot summer. The nights were cool, never sultry. They generally burnt poplar for fuel. The hotelkeeper told him he paid 3s. for a small cart-load.

DR. JAMES LYNCH'S EVIDENCE.

James Lynch, examined—He was born at Niagara, but went to settle at Red River in June 1869. He is a doctor, but went to Red River with intention of farming. He settled on the shores of Lake Manitoba in the vicinity of White Mud River. The prairie burns every fall. There are capital fish in Manitoba Lake. Climate resembles that of Canada, except that in summer nights are cool, and weather never sultry. It is a good country for settlement: exceedingly healthy; just such a country as he would like to make his home in. The wheat crop is excellent. He does not know anything about frosts doing any severity in September. They make fences with poplar poles. Fuel question may shortly be a difficulty. He saw a great many ducks in the country, and there are a good many elk by the Assiniboine. There are plenty of prairie hens which are larger than the Western—a cross between the quail and the partridge. The water of the rivers is wholesome but that of the lakes contains a good deal of sediment. The horses are poor. The cattle are large. He sees no obstacles to the settlement of Red River that may not be surmounted. Timber may be grown for fuel. He continued :—"I intend going back, and will invite my friends to accompany me. I went to the Red River Territory with the intention of becoming a settler, if from what I saw of it I considered it a desirable place of residence and favourable to the occupation I designed to follow, that of stock-breeding and farming. I saw the country with the eyes of a practical farmer—of a Canadian who had travelled considerably over this continent and visited others of the colonies. I saw it during an exceptionally unfavorable summer and autum and an unusually severe winter. I had ample opportunities of observing those peculiarities which must strike every stranger visiting the country for the first time, and I unhesitatingly give it as my sincerest conviction, that as regards climate, judging from what is prominently noticeable in the general good health and fine physique of the natives, and from my own personal experience, it even possesses many advantages over Canada. The fertility and inexhaustible nature of the soil are superior to that of any other part of the world."

ARTHUR HAMILTON'S EVIDENCE.

Arthur Hamilton, examined—Was born in New Brunswick, but lived the greater part of his life in Hamilton. He testified to the richness of the soil and stated, he found the summer pleasant, the winter cool and clear. He saw some frost in the woods in September, but he was told that the frosts are earlier in the woods and swamps than in the open prairie. He was favorably impressed with the half-breeds. They are willing, good workers. The climate and country are magnificent.

MAJOR BOLTON'S EVIDENCE

Major Bolton, examined—Is a native of Ontario, Went to Red River in August, 1869. He was engaged on Col. Dennis' survey. After leaving Pembina they enter a prairie country. As they got near Assinniboine they saw clumps of woods. The principal part of the land, from the boundary line to Assinniboine, is fit for settlement. Distance is about 64 miles. About Stinking River the country is really beautiful. Rose trees and strawberries grow in luxuriance on higher parts of prairie to which he had refered. The grass is very nutritious, and during winter horses scrape the snow away to get it. He saw the first well to the north on a stock farm. It supplied 250 to 300 head of cattle. This well was 25 feet deep. As he went north he found the country more wooded and more stony. There are no stones on the prairie. He had not seen any fruit trees on the prairie, but one or two gentlemen had lately put out apple tree and they appeared to be doing well. The production in the harvest fields on the banks of the river was certainly wonderful last summer. But the grasshoppers have done much harm, and the blackbirds are injurious. The crop was large— sufficient to last the settlement for two years. The yield is far superior to tha of Upper Canada. The grasshoppers have done damage for the last six or seven years more or less. The houses are generally made of oak logs. From the parts of the country he has seen it compares favorably with Ontario. Sheep and pigs both flourish in the country. Sometimes there is a superfluity of the latter, and people have had to drown them in the river, for there is only a imited market for surplus production. He intends to go back.

DR. SCHULTZ'S EVIDENCE.

Dr. John Schultz examined—He is a doctor of medicine, and has resided at Fort Garry for nearly ten years. He was born in Canada, and formerly resided in Essex County. He has practiced medecine, and been engaged in fur trading. He has been all through the country between Red River and Lake of the Woods, and he has been some 70 miles on the Assinhiboine. The winter is colder than Ontario, but with the same clothes that he wore in Essex, he suffered less from the cold. The cold and snow are very dry. The average depth of the snow is 18 inches. He has known the thermometer fall as low as —45°. Snow generally begins to fall on the 10th of November. Spring opens about Easter Day. Ploughing is all done in the spring. There is not much seed put in before the 22nd or 23rd of April. The heat of the summer is not extreme. July is the hottest month. They have not much wet weather. He has noticed small patches of Alkali deposits on the prairies. They occur in the neighborhood of Lake Manitoba. The cattle go and lick them up. He has never seen any country superior for settlement, and he has been in Wisconsin, Iowa, Minnesota, and Illinois. The alluvial soil is over a footh in depth. There is below it a sort of clay mixed with sand, called white mud. The White Mud River, so named from the character of the soil, is one of the best districts for agricultural purposes. He has seen coal brought from the upper part of Assinniboinne, which appeared to burn well. As you go further from the rivers you meet with the Buffalo grass, which is not so long, but more nutritious than the ordinary herbage. The average yield of grain in this country is greater than in Canada. Last year the yield of wheat in some parts was 40 bushels to the acre. The average is not much over 30. It weighs over 60 lbs. to the bushel. Oats are 32 lbs. to the bushel. Barley turns out equally well. Vegetables, and especially potatoes, yield very well. In the town the price of 5-8ths of an ordinary Canadian cord of wood would be $1. Hay is 5s. a cart load. Cattle come in about Christmas, and are turned out early. He would recommed immigrants to go to this country to settle, in preference to Canada. The country is healthy. There is an absence of fevers and epidemics. Thk immigrant should take agricultural implements with him. A man with from £50 to £100stg. would have no difficulty in making a satisfactory living. Fish are very abundant. Lake trout and white fish can be caught in winter. There is a demand for labor in the harvest season, but as a rule every man does his own work. There are mowing and reaping machines in the country. It is his intention to return to the country.

CHARLES GARRETT'S EVIDENCE.

Charles Garrett examined—He has lived for upwards of eleven years at Red River. He previously resided in the neighborhood of Toronto and Lake Simcoe. He has been living at a place called Sturgeon Creek, on the Assiniboine, seven miles north of the town of Winnipeg, where he has [farmed for the last eight years. Receding from the river the soil is good—a mixture of mould and clay without a boulder. Ploughs that go through it are hard to clean. Has been to Lake Manitoba and seen the Salt Licks, which are four or five acres as a rule. Timothy grows well, but the dry springs are against the growth of the clover. He has seen clover stand for years. The wheat crops are not injured by cold winds or by mil-dew. He has seen the harvest as early as the first week in August. Frost takes possession of the ground about the 15th October, and farming commences again on the 15th of April. The grass is very rank, and cattle eat the grass as soon as the snow is off the ground, on April 1st. He has learnt from persons beyond Portage La Prairie and north of the Saskatchewan, that the country west of Portage La Prairie to Fort Ellice, and up to the Qu'Appelle, is admirable for agricultural purposes—in fact it has always been considered the finest portion of the country. He raises wheat ; gets 22 to 25 bushels return for one sown. Oats are a safe crop, and yield 55 bushels to the acre. He thinks the country favorable for immigrants' He never knew one more favorable for farming. He heard it stated that by the Mackenzie River, in the more distant North-west, the spring is a fortnight earlier than with them, and that it is the finest part of the country for settlement. He has seen coal from the upper part of the Assiniboine, three days journey, or eighty or ninety miles from Portage La Prairie. House building is about twice as dear in Red River as Canada. Timber is more expensive, ac nails are twenty cents a pound. Lumber is $40 a thousand ; lime is 18 cents bushel, and labour in proportion. Shingles are $4 per M. Stoves are chief imported from Canada and dear. He paid £14 sterling for one, which he coul have bought for $50 or $55 in Ontario. Boots, shoes, and woollen goods con from Canada in bond. An emigrant should buy a waggon and horses at S Pauls, to transport himself and his family, and his plough and agricultur instruments that he must take with him. A light steel plough is the best fc the soil. It might be better to take oxen, as they are always worth the price. Best time to go is latter part of May and month of October, It woul take a team about twenty days from St. Cloud. By going in May he can buil a house and plough the ground ready for spring. They do not plough deer Carpenters are in demand. They have been getting 10s. a day. Plasterer the same. For stonemasons there is no demand. Immigration has been in creasing since he went there. The educational facilities are good.

CHARLES MAIR'S EVIDENCE.

Charles Mair, examined—Is a native of Lanark, Canada. Went to Rec River two years ago, as paymaster on the Fort Garry section of the Red Rive Road. He is familiar with the country from a point 60 miles east from For Garry, to 120 or 130 miles west. He has crossed the Assiniboine at two differen points—one 130 miles west of Fort Garry—and knows the country betweel that river and Pembina and St. Joseph—half-breed settlements on the fron tier. It is a beautiful rolling country and well timbered. Receding from th rivers the country is rich. There is wood enough for ordinary purposes. One tenth of the land is covered with wood, though it is small. There are no many lakes or streams. Waggons could be taken over every part of it There are plenty of birds. All the Canadian kinds, besides the magpie, which are very common. There is a species of small hare in the country. There are geese, including the white Arctic goose. Has seen all the aquatic and land birds, except woodcock and quail. There are squirrels, but they are smaller than in Canada. He has been over the country between Manitoba Lake and Assiniboine. It is a fine country. He has taken up handfuls of vegetable loam at the depth of six feet on the prairies. He has seen coal deposits. It is used at Fort Edmonton and at Fort Garry in the forges. The deposits have been on fire several times. It is considered good coal. It is brought from the Souris River, 180 miles west. The Assinniboine is navigable as far as Portage a Prairie by steamboat. But it is shallow and bed sandy and shifting. It light be dredged. He has known as many as 65 or 70 bushels of wheat grown othe acre; the average yield, I have neard, placed at 40. I may say that a armer going from Canada to Red River ecnsiders he has found a better country than he has left. On the other hand, a Red River farmer is disappointed with the soil of the Western States; he considers it thinner and poorer. He has known wheat grow on the same soil for forty years and succeed. The armers never use manure. Fish are plentiful. He did not find the cold effect him so much as in Canada. He intends to return to the country. The country is admirably adapted for sheep. There is no danger from wolves or other wild animals.

STATEMENTS BY THE UNITED STATES CONSUL AT WINNIPEG.

The subjoined letter from Mr. James W. Taylor, the United States Consul at Manitoba, is copied from a Western United States newspaper. It is given here as the testimony of an American, in official position, for the information of his own people as to the capabilities and productions of Manitoba:—

"U. S. CONSULATE,
"WINNIPEG, B.N.A., Sept. 11, 1872.

"SIR,—In response to your communication, requesting samples of the agricultural products of Manitoba for exhibition at the Minnesota State Fair, I forward specimens of the wheat crops of 1871, a parcel of winter wheat harvested in 1872, some Indian corn and oats, and a few vegetables.

"The season here is fully two weeks later than in Minnesota. Your State Fair is earlier than usual, and the Manitoba crops are not yet threshed. A month later it will be convenient to send a full list of the grain and vegetables of the current year.

"I will add a few words of explanation in regard to the samples herewith forwarded.

"The wheat produced by John Flett (one half bushel) was imported forty years since from England, where it was a fall or winter variety, but in course of its acclimation it has become a spring wheat, known as English.

"It shows some signs of deterioration from constant cultivation on the same farms for nearly half a century, yet a parcel forwarded by me to the Department of Agriculture at Washington was so much esteemed that the Commissioner proposes to circulate a considerable quantity in the United States as

'Manitoba Spring Wheat.' Mr. Flett's farm is on the east bank of Red River, three miles north of Fort Garry.

"I send one-third bushel spring wheat from the farm of John Matheson, in Kildoonan (the Scotch parish), four miles north of Winnipeg, which is mainly the 'English.' A third variety of spring wheat may be termed 'Manitoba Spring,' the seed being sent by Mr. N. W. Kitson to Hon. James McKay in the winter of 1868, one-and-a-quarter bushels of which in 1869 produced 44 bushels on one acre, and has since averaged 30 bushels per acre for field cultivation.

"You will notice a few heads of bearded wheat from the farm of John Matheson, second, of Kildoonan. They are from a field of spring wheat in 1871, which bore a considerable crop this year, although left fallow.

"I also send some heads of the 'English Spring.'

"I invite your particular attention to the specimen of 'Fultz Winter, grown in St. Boniface, by Mr. Jean Mayer, from seed furnished me by Mr. Fred. Watts, U. S. Commissioner of Agriculture. It was sown October 2, 1871, and harvested August 10, 1872. When the snow disappeared this spring the plants were barely visible, but they came to great perfection, and the yield was at the extraordinary rate of 72 bushels per acre. Results signally remarkable attended the cultivation of the 'Fultz' wheat by Hon. James McKay, of St. James Parish, and Mr. John Matheson.

"Encouraged by these results, the U. S. Department of Agriculture are about to distribute through this Province a liberal supply of Tappahanock and Forzelle Winter Wheat and Winter Rye.

"I am gratified to observe that Commissioner Watts will attend and address the Minnesota State Fair. May I ask that you will personally communicate to him the thanks of the agriculturists of Manitoba for the distribution of new and valuable seeds in this Province.

"The new ears of corn sent are the squaw variety grown at the mission of Northern Minnesota. It only reaches the height of three feet, but is very prolific. This specimen was planted by Hugh Polson, of Kildoonan, May 15th, and gathered September 4th.

"The sheaf of 'Fultz' winter wheat is sent to indicate the growth and appearance of the plant.

"I have no doubt that the productions of the distri far north of the line of your road will compare favorably with the results of agriculture in similar reas of North Europe.

"I am, Sir,

"Yours truly,

"JAMES W. TAYLOR."

LETTER FROM ARCHDEACON McLEAN.

This letter of Mr. Taylor was submitted by the Department of Agriculture to the Ven. Archdeacon McLean, on the occasion of a visit to Ottawa, in order to obtain his opinion, as a resident, as to the accuracy of the statements contained in it. He replied in the following letter :

"OTTAWA, 10th February, 1873.

JOHN LOWE, Esq.,

Secretary Department of Agriculture.

"SIR,—In reference to the letter of Jas. W. Taylor, Esq., U. S. Consul as Winnipeg, on the subject of Manitoba wheat, I beg to say that the statements contained in it relative to the average yield per acre, agree fully with the results of my own observation during nearly a seven years residence in Manitoba. There is no doubt at all that forty bushels of wheat can be got in Manitoba, with ordinary care in farming. My observations have reference only to Spring wheat. I have not seen any efforts made to cultivate Fall wheat, although I know no reason why they should not be successful.

"With regard to ordinary kitchen vegetables, I do not think it possible to surpass the products of Manitoba.

"About the first week of October 1 attended an Agricultural show of the products of the Province, held at Fort Garry. I do not remember ever seeing so fine a display of vegetables anywhere. The potatoes, turnips, cabbages, beets and onions, were of a size and apparent quality that indicated the very richest soil.

"Let me take the opportunity of reminding you that Manitoba is afterall but a very small portion of the Great Fertile Belt of our Dominion.

"The Valley of the Upper Assiniboine with those of its affluents, the Rapid River or Little Saskatchewan, the Shed River, the Swan, and other rivers—and the valley of the Saskatchewan—stretching westward to the Rocky Mountains, contains millions upon millions of soil as rich as that of the best in Manitoba, with a magnificent climate, and every requisite for securing the health and material prosperity of a vast population.

" I can speak with as much certainty of the climate and soil of those po:
tions of the Fertile Belt, that I have not seen, as of Manitoba, where I hav
lived for years.

" I have made it my business to converse with Missionaries, Hudson Ba.
Officers, and natives of the country, who have lived for long periods in th
various sections. I have carried on this practice for a series of years, takin
notes of the conversations. I have compared from time to time one man
statement with that of another, and I am to-day thoroughly convinced that th
Saskatchewan Valley is destined to be the great field for emigration.

" The land in the Saskatchewan valley is on the whole very similar to tha
of Red River, though not quite so level.

" The thermometer falls lower in winter, but as there is very seldom an;
high wind, the cold is not much felt.

" The severe frost pulverises the ground, and renders it easily ploughed ir
spring.

" Wheat grows there in great perfection, and is ready to cut from the middle to the end of August.

" The risk of early frost is chiefly confined to the neighborhood of swampy
flats. In general there is but little risk on the high ground.

" The grasshoppers that from time to time visited Red River, have never
yet done any serious damage in the Saskatchewan Valley. In 1866 they came to
Carleton, but did not spread beyond fifteen miles east. The Red River Valley
has been exposed to the grasshoppers in common with the prairie lands of the
United State. We have reason to believe that the liability will cease, or at
least decrease very much, when a large section of the country is under cultivation.

" I remain, Sir,

" Yours truly,

" JOHN MCLEAN, D.D., D.C.L.,

" Archdeacon of Manitoba."

STATEMENT OF MR. G. B. SPENCE.

The following are notes of an an interview of Mr. G. B. Spence, Collector
of Customs at Winnipeg, Manitoba, with the late Minister of Agriculture, at
his office, on the 11th February, 1873. They are given here as further evidence
respecting the productions of the soil and climate of Manitoba :—

In answer to a question from the Minister, Mr. Spence said he had been in Manitoba since the 22nd December, 1870.

MINISTER—What time does Spring begin there ?

MR. SPENCE—In 1871 the Spring opened about the 1st April. The river is navigable about 23rd of April. In 1872 the Spring set in somewhere about ten days later. The first steamer went down early in May.

Q. What time do farmers sow wheat there ?

A. They sow in April or May, from about the 15th or 20th of April to the 5th or 20th May. The Spring is shorter than it is here, and sets in without any breaks.

Q. What quantity of wheat do they raise to the acre ?

A. They raise from thirty to sixty-three bushels to the acre, Forty bushels is the average.

Q. What is the usual weight per bushel ?

A. Sixty-two lbs. I have been told by persons who have seen it, that wheat can be cultivated for forty years, continuously, without manure.

Q. What about oats and barley, and root crops ?

A. The barley sown there is very fine ; the oats are not so good. Buck wheat has never been tried. Root crops are extraordinary. Cabbage and cauliflower grow almost of their own accord. Cabbage grow to a very large size. Potatoes aand turnips are very fine, also mangolds. Sugar beet has never been grown, but some parties think of trying it. Tomatoes, if they were to take the same trouble as in this country, would answer well. Very little attention is paid to scientific farming. The grasses have not been thoroughly tested ; have seen small patches of timothy, which were very good. The wild grasses are very good for pasturage. There are what are called hay farms.

Q. Do farmers house their cattle ?

A. Hundreds of cattle are never housed, and look far better than those you see come out of barns.

Q. Is the climate equal to that of Minnesota ?

A. The climate is much the same.

Q. The soil ?

A. Yes. The soil is believed to be better than that of Minnesota. I believe there is no country where the soil is equal to it.

Q. What time do they usually cut the grass ?

A. At the latter part of July and beginning of August.

Q. What time does winter set in ?

A. Winter usually sets in about the 1st of December, sometimes a little earlier. The snow lasts till the 1st of April.

Q. How many months could you plough in ?

A. Five, if not six. Part of April, May, June, July, August, September, and part of October.

Q. As to the cold in winter ?

A. The air is drier than it is here, and the cold is not felt so much,

Q. What about summer ?

A. The greater part of the summer is pretty hot. The thermometer ranges about ninety degrees : have seen it go up to ninety-six degrees. There is not much rain.

Q. Supposing you were a man without means and with a family, would you go there ?

A. A man without means has a better chance there than he would have by going into bush land. Fuel is more accessible there than in the prairie. If you go back fifty or sixty miles you come to timber lands.

NARRATIVE OF A JOURNEY

—TO—

MANITOBA,

BY JACOB Y. SHANTZ,

——o——

The following narrative of a journey to Manitoba was written in 1873 by Mr. Jacob Y. Shantz, a German Menonite, resident in Berlin, Ontario.

Mr. Shantz, at the request of the Department of Agriculture, visited Ottawa, in company with Mr. Bernard Warkentin, a German Menonite from Berdiansk, Russia, in November last, as interpreter.

The object of Mr. Warkentin in visiting Canada was to find a place suitable for the settlement of Menonites who contemplate an emigration, *en masse*, from Russia.

At the request of the Department of Agriculture, he, with Mr. Shantz, visited Manitoba.

Mr. Shantz states that in writing a narrative of the journey, he has been moved by the simple desire to set down the facts with the utmost possible accuracy, and with truthfulness on which all may rely.

He wrote as follows :—

MANITOBA AND THE NORTH-WEST.

On the 5th November, 1872, Mr. Bernard Warkentin, cf Russia, and myself left Berlin by the Grand Trunk Railway to Detroit (*en route* for the Province of Manitoba) ; thence by the Southern Michigan Railway to Chicago ; thence to St. Paul, Minnesota, and by the Lake Superior and Mississippi Railway to Duluth ; thence by the Northern Pacific Railway to Moorehead on the Red River, a place situated immediately on the boundary line between the States

2

of Minnesota and Dacotah, from which place we proceeded to Pembina on the borders of Manitoba.

Entering that Province, we travelled a distance of 72 miles by stage to Fort Garry and Winnipeg, the latter being situated contiguous to the Fort, and rising place. A railroad is now in course of construction to Pembina, which will be completed during the present year. We might have saved about 2 miles had we taken the route via Breckenridge, but in order to avoid travelling by stage, we took the longer route by railway. From Pembina we travelled about 50 miles along the Red River—a portion of the Province as yet entire unsettled, with the exception of a few stations scattered every 15 or 20 miles where relays of horses and refreshments for passengers are provided. Passing this district the Half-bred settlements commence, small white houses with stables attached dotting the scene, and which become more numerous the nearer we approach the Fort.

Seven miles from Fort Garry we passed a grist-mill; the houses present a better appearance, the farms being well fenced, and the Assiniboine River was reached, a tributary of the Red River. The former stream is navigable for a distance of 60 miles or more, and though not wide is deep. Red River is navigable some 230 miles to the south and 30 to the north, where it empties into Lake Winnipeg, with an expanse of about 1,000 feet at the Town of Winnipeg. Fort Garry, the principal trading post of the Hudson Bay Company contains a small fortress with a garrison of soldiers. A large warehouse belonging to the Company, is situated on the River's bank, in which six clerks are employed. There is also a telegraph office, and several two story houses around the fort. Work had been commenced upon the foundations of a new hotel to be erected this year at a cost of $14,000.

At a distance of about a quarter of a mile or so lies the Town of Winnipeg the capital of the Province, only founded a few years ago, but which already contains 12 stores, 5 hotels, and a large saw-mill, capable of cutting from ten to fifteen thousand feet of lumber per day. There are also a planing mill, and four printing offices. The houses are mostly frame, brick being the exception though they are now being manufactured there. Stone and lime are procurable within six miles. The roads, as well as the streets, are in bad order, with very little sidewalk, but the building operations continually going on, and teaming in connection therewith will cut them up for some time to come.

On the eastern side of Red River lies the village of St. Boniface containing a Roman Catholic Cathedral, Church of England, Presbyterian Church, and a school-house. Further down the river is St. John (Church of England) College. After seeing Winnipeg, we started for the Indian Mission, about 60 miles to the north-west. For a distance of some two miles are the houses of the Half-breeds, after which nothing was to be seen but the unbroken prairie, till we arrived at "Cattle Farm," 20 miles distant, where we saw 100 head of cattle grazing. The farm-buildings consisted of a small dwelling-house with out buildings, and a stack of hay containing about 100 tons. When we left there on the 23rd November, the cattle were still in the fields, and the pasture was good. For the rest of the distance to Indian Mission, the country changes, the prairie being dotted here and there with belts of woodland known as " bluffs," containing from one half to ten acres, for the most part poplar. This timber is used by the half-breeds for building purposes, for fences, and for fuel. On arrival at the Mission we found about twenty families of French half-breeds, who lived by hunting and fishing. Here we met Mr. William Wagner, Provincial Land Surveyor, who takes great interest in the encouragement of immigration to Manitoba. Immigrants arriving, especially Germans, would do well to apply to this gentleman for information as to the most profitable and desirable lands on which to settle.

Leaving the Indian Mission we journeyed south-west along the eastern shore of Lake Manitoba, and found fine prairie land there, dotted as before with "bluffs." For 40 miles we travelled without seeing a house till we reached a spot called "Poplar Point," on the Assinniboine, where we found a farm of about 90 acres under cultivation, belonging to a Mr. Taylor, who owns a large number of cattle. In the vicinity is a settlement of English half-breeds, chiefly Protestants, and possessing three churches, English, Presbyterian and Methodist. Proceeding still further westward along the banks of the River, which are settled by small farmers, we arrived at "High Bluffs" a place with three churches and a school house. Here we staid at a farm belonging to a Mr. Allcock, an Englishman, who came here from Ontario three years ago. He showed us as fine a sample of spring wheat as I had ever seen, and told us that he had harvested 40 bushels to the acre. He also exhibited a splendid sample of oats, flax seed, potatoes, turnips, cabbage and other vegetables.

Seven miles further on, in a westerly direction, we came to the village of

" Portage La Prairie," with six stores, a grist mill, four saw mills, and quite
large number of mechanics. We next visited Messrs. Grant and Mackenz
whose farms lie about eight miles distant from "Portage La Prairie," both
whom came from the Province of Ontario. Mr. Grant showed us a sample
wheat which had turned out 30 bushels to the acre, and some very fine oats. I
potatoes also were of a very large size and superior quality, such as I ha
never seen surpassed. Mr. Mackenzie's wheat yielded 32 bushels to the acr
He also showed us about 100 bushels of onions, measuring from two to fl
and a half inches in diameter. The turnips also were of a very large size,
which three would weigh 60 lbs. He stated that he had taken 1,200 bushels
potatoes off of four and three quarter acres of land—prairie land broken up, a:
the potatoes ploughed under. He also showed us young apple trees which :
had raised from seed, that looked very thrifty. This gentleman also possess
a herd of ninety head of cattle, amongst which I remarked a full-bred Durha
bull, and some Durham cows. I am thus particular in mentioning all I saw
this farm, that the reader may form some idea of the richness of the soil. T!
distance from "Poplar Point" to Mr. Mackenzie's farm is about 22 miles up t!
Assinniboine River, along which there is a good strip of timber, and the lar
well settled, partly by English half-breeds and immigrants from Ontario.

Returning to "Poplar Point," we resumed our journey in an easterly dire
tion by the main road towards Winnipeg, and at a distance of 12 miles, v
reached St. Paul's Mission. Six miles further we came to Pigeon Lake, or
mile distant from which is the Hudson Bay Company's Post, known as "Whl
Horse Post," where the Company carries on farming on an extensive scal
9,870 bushels of grain having been raised in 1871 on two hundred and ninet
acres of land. The Company also maintain here about 500 head of cattl
Twelve miles further we came to Headingley, a small village, and four mile
distant from that is Sturgeon Creek, where there is a steam mill and distiller.
Passing, "Silver Heights," where the Hon. Donald A. Smith, Governor of th
Hudson's Bay Company, resides, we came to St. Paul's Church (Church
England), and after a further distance of five miles, reached again our startir
point. Our road lay on the north side of, and along the Assiniboine River ; th
soil consists of good rich prairie land, and belts of timber, consisting of Elm
Basswood, Ash, and Poplar.

Leaving Winnipeg again in a north-easterly direction, we proceeded alon

Red River to the Hudson Bay Company's Post, known as the Stone Fort, here there is a small garrison. The whole distance from Winnipeg to the rt is thickly settled. Respecting the weather, whilst travelling in the States Minnesota and Dacotah, from the 10th November to the 1st December it owed continually with drift, although the snow was not over eight inches ep on the plains ; on reaching the Manitoba line, however, we found very tle snow, and on arrival at Fort Garry on 17th November, there was not ough snow to cover the ground. From the 18th to the 28th November there is no snow of any consequence in Manitoba, and on the 1st December leaving rt Garry on our return we had beautiful weather, travelling by stage, on heels, 140 miles. The further south we came the more snow we found, till on ir arrival at St. Paul, it was fully a foot in depth. This confirmed the stateent made by the people in Manitoba that they do not experience as much ow as falls in Minnesota and Dacotah. Apparently the further westward u travel in Manitoba, the less snow is met with, and the milder is the mate.

ZE, GROWTH AND DEVELOPMENT OF WINNIPEG, THE CAPITAL OF MANITOBA
AND THE NORTH WEST.

A general desire being felt to know the exact increase of the population of innipeg during the last summer, much speculation has existed, based upon kinds of random suppositions. Judging from the ordinary indications of de and building, few towns can boast a more rapid growth. In the Fall of 70 the population was 300, whilst in the Fall of 1871 it had increased to 700, and the Fall of last year, a careful enumeration made showed a population of 167, thus giving an increase of nearly 800 during the past year. The number houses erected during last building season were stores, dwellings and wareuses of one story high, thirty-four; of one-and-a-half stories, one; making tal in all of 124 new buildings. In addition to this there are now under conact a brick hotel to contain 100 rooms, for Mr. A. M. Brown; the Canadian acific Hotel, with a frontage of 90 feet, and to contain 100 rooms; whilst numeris stores and warehouses together with private residences are being erected. ere remains to be mentioned the Receiver General's Office, Custom House d Post Office to be erected by the Dominion Government, at an average cost

With respect to wages, although varying according to circumstances and place, the average prices may be set down as follows; Carpenters, $3.50 per day; bricklayers and masons, $1 per day; painters $3.50, and labourers $2.50 per day. These rates of wages, though higher perhaps than elsewhere, are not the only advantage, for the sober and industrious may, out of the savings of one or two months, secure, by making their first payment, a lot and a home of their own.

The market rates, as far as we could ascertain them, where the supply is so irregular and uncertain, were : wheat, $1.25 per bushel; oats, $1.00 per bushel; barley, $1.10 per bushel; potatoes, 62 cents; onions, $2.00; carrots, 75 cents; turnips 50 cents, and beets 50 cents per bushel. Hay was selling from $7.00 to $8.00 per ton; butter, 30 cents per lb; eggs, 30 cents per dozen; beef, 12½ cents per lb; lamb the same; veal, 20 cents; pork, 20 cents; and fresh fish about 5 cents per lb. Board ranges from $5.00 to $9.00 per week, though many young men save money by boarding themselves.

STINKING RIVER SETTLEMENT.

This settlement is best reached by way of Headingley and thence south over the Pembina trail which crosses the Stinking River, near the upper end of the settlement. The land on both sides of the river is nearly occupied through the extent of townships 8 and 9 in the second range. The settlers are for the most part from Central Canada.

Stinking River contains water at all seasons, clear and good, except at a few points where salt springs affect it for short distances; good water can, however, be had anywhere by digging to a depth of a dozen or twenty feet.

Both banks of the river are fringed with oak and poplar of good size, in sufficient quantities for settlement use, which increase in size and density as the river is ascended.

The prairie, on either side, consists of a black loam, easily cultivated and of sufficient undulation from the numerous gullies leading to the river to be well drained, an important point towards early cultivation and quick growth. North of the river is an unlimited supply of marsh hay, the spontaneous growth of the marsh which extends to the southeast over parts of two Townships.

BOYNE RIVER SETTLEMENT.

The River Boyne takes its rise in the Pembina Mountains, and is about 50 miles long, flowing in a north-easterly direction until it loses itself in the reat marsh, mentioned before as extending to the vicinity of the Stinking River Settlement. Its banks are, for the greater part, lined with a fringe of heavy oak timber, to the depth of from a quarter to half a mile, till towards the mountain It extends into a forest of a number of miles wide; on the edge of he marsh, however, poplar is the principal timber met with.

The present occupants point with pride to the substantial character of their improvements, their houses being well built and commodious. Some of the largest enclosures in the Province are to be met with in this settlement, it being no unusual thing to see a field of 100 acres, of 60 acres, and 50 acres respectively, used for pasturage, the trouble of fencing being amply repaid by the certainty of always finding the cattle when wanted. The majority of the settlers here are Canadians, and the land is taken up for a distance of five miles east and west; beyond that, however, there is an abundance of land equally good, embracing the richest prairie land, with wood, water and hay.

The natural advantages of the Boyne district for the raising of cattle, with its abundant supply of water, fodder and shelter, has attracted the attention of the Messrs. Grant, of Sturgeon Creek, and Campbell Brothers, from Ontario, both of whom have considerable droves of cattle fattening on the prairie. The unlimited supply of acorns which strew the ground in the oak-woods, would suffice to feed a large herd of swine.

In the Boyne River settlement there are about thirty families.

VICTORIA.

This settlement commences about three miles north of Stony Mountain, but the latter term would not, in any other than a level country, bo so applied. It is a ridge some 70 or 100 feet above the surrounding level, of about three miles in length and from a quarter to half a mile in width. The eastern side is a gentle slope, but the western is broken, some portions of it being precipitous. It is covered with a fine growth of poplar. The ridge is composed mostly of Limestone rocks, which, where exposed to view, appear to run in layers of from a foot to twenty inches in thickness. No better building stone can possibly be found, and the supply is practically inexhaustible.

THE WESTERN DISTRICT OF MANITOBA.

The traveller, pursuing his journey westwards from Winnipeg, would say that all the land which meets the eye is good farming land, but it is only as he reaches Poplar Point that he sees the best of it.

The land stretching from there to Rat Creek, and from the River Assiniboine to Lake Manitoba, connot be excelled for agricultural purposes. Practical men, who have viewed the wheat lands of California, the extensive plains of Australia, and the wide-spreading prairies of the Western States, agree on this point.

The river lots from Poplar Point to Portage la Prairie were, for the most part, taken up ten years ago by native inhabitants from the Red River Settlement below Winnipeg, who have sold out again in turn to Canadians and Hudson Bay Company employees. The land outside of the river lots is also rapidly filling up.

The statements that I have made with regard to the enormous yield of cereals and roots, are not over estimated. As a further proof of this, in October, 1871, one quart of Fall wheat was sown not far from Winnipeg, the same was harvested in August, 1872, and produced the very best sample of grain at the rate of 72 bushels per acre, which was exhibited at the Minnesota State Fair, and pronounced the best sample on exhibition.

There is stated to be a settlement on the Lake of the Woods road, on the Dawson route, with a beautiful park-like appearance, abutting on the River Seine, in Township X, Range 4, in which several families from Ontario are settled, whose land must shortly become very valuable, being within ten miles of the town of Winnipeg.

Springfield, another settlement in an easterly direction from Winnipeg, now presents quite a thriving appearance, and contains from 60 to 70 families. Near it is another settlement known as Sunnyside, containing about 30 families, nearly all from Ontario. The half-breeds are settled for the most part along the Assiniboine and Red Rivers.

The reader will observe, from the above remarks, that it is not an unsettled country to which he is invited to go and make himself a home on a free grant, but that there are plenty of settlements which he can join. Advantages are afforded in Manitoba and the North West that a new settler in the Western States, though lying further to the South, could not possess, of which I will now make mention.

First. In Manitoba the land is principally prairie, requiring no clearing for agricultural purposes, although timber is to be found in sufficient abundance for building purposes, fencing, and fuel. In addition to the latter there are the large coal fields further west on the Saskatchewan River.

Wherever settlements have been established both grist and sawmills are to be met with.

Secondly. In the Western States the Railway Companies own the lands from 10 to 20 miles on either side of their respective roads, which settlers cannot obtain as Free Grants, but for which they have to pay from $2.50 upwards per acre, according to locality. In the Province of Manitoba, however, the settler can at present make his choice of any lots which are not yet taken up; he can always join a settlement, and need never become isolated.

Thirdly. There are good prospects of both railway and water communication before long, the facilities for the latter being especially good, the Province abounding in rivers and lakes which extend through the North West to the very base of the Rocky Mountains, and eastwards to Lake Superior, with the exception of a distance of one hundred and fifty-three miles, as stated by Mr. Wagner, which would require a canal to establish complete water communication.

A steamboat belonging to the Hudson Bay Company already runs on the Saskatchewan for a distance of 600 miles. There is also an outlet through the States by way of Red River, which is navigable from Fort Garry through Minnesota and Dacotah, a distance of 288 miles to Breckenridge, where a branch of the Northern Pacific Railway from St. Paul, 216 miles, distant, crosses the river. There is also a railway direct from St. Paul to Pembina on the boundary line, which will be completed and in running order during the coming summer, and which it is thought will be extended to Fort Garry.

Fourthly. Another inducement which Manitoba has to offer settlers is, if the free grant of land to which they are entitled is not sufficient, more can be procured at one dollar per acre, whereas in the Western States, even beyond the limits of Railway Company's Lands, the price is one dollar and twenty cents per acre.

Fifthly. Although Manitoba lies to the north of Minnesota and Dacotah, the cold is neither so extreme, nor the snow fall as heavy as in the latter States, and the changes in the weather are not sudden, as in Kansas and Nebraska States, still further south. In Manitoba during winter the weather though cold is regular, the air dry and healthy. The snow is seldom more than from one to one and a half feet deep, and further west on the Saskatchewan it is said to be even less than that.

COST OF TRANSPORT.

The cost of transportation for Emigrants from Toronto to Manitoba is as follows :—

Mr. Shantz here gives the cost of transport by the Dawson Route, but as this is elsewhere given in this pamphlet in official form it is omitted.)

The above route (the Dawson) can only be used in the summer season, and till the ice sets in in the fall. There are several other routes to Manitoba from Canada, which are more convenient but at the same time more expensive. One route is from any point on Lake Huron, whence steamboats start, to Duluth on the North Westerly shore of Lake Superior, thence by Northern Pacific Railway to Glynden, 212 miles distant. From this point a line branches northwardly 152 miles to Pembina on the boundary line, the remainder of the distance to Fort Garry being completed by stages or steam-boats on the Red River.

Another route is by the Grand Trunk Railway from Toronto to Detroit, and thence by way of Chicago and St. Paul to Breckenridge on the Red River, where steamers run in summer to Fort Garry, some 500 miles distant, or if by land, taking the stage route from Breckenridge, 288 miles. This route costs through from Toronto, first class, $50 to $60, according to the season, the fare being lower in summer than in winter.

A question frequently asked is

WHAT KIND OF PEOPLE ARE THE HALF-BREEDS ?

To briefly state their history then, in the year 1630 a company was formed in London under the direction of Prince Rupert for the purpose of prosecuting the fur trade in the region of country surrounding Hudson's Bay. This company obtained a charter from King Charles II. granting to them and their successors, under the name of "The Governor and Company of adventurers trading into Hudson's Bay," the sole right of trading in all the country watered by rivers flowing into the Hudson's Bay—the charter also authorized them to build and fit out men-of-war, establish forts, and to prevent any other Company from carrying on trade with the natives in their territories, and requiring that they should do all in their power to promote discovery. This Company frequently brought men from England and Scotland as employes for their trading posts, and for the purpose of hunting and trapping—these intermarrying with the native Indians produced the race of people now known as the English half-breeds or properly speaking half Indians.

In the year 1733 another Company was formed, composed of French Canadians from Montreal, who commenced the fur trade further East and North of Lake Superior, without any permission from the Goverument or otherwise. This Company, it is said, at one time employed five thousand men. At length trouble arose between the Hudson's Bay Company and the French Company; and frequent quarrels arose, sometimes ending in bloodshed.

In the year 1821 the two rival Companies amalgamated. The French Canadians also intermarried with the native Indians, and their descendants were called French half-breeds—this happened over a century ago—so that all these half-breeds have become, as it were, a distinct race of people.

They are a civilized class of people. I have been amongst them as a stranger, have boarded and lodged with them, and I have invariably found them very obliging and hospitable, and to their honour be it said, I saw none of them as rough and wicked as some of our own class of Canadians. They have schools and churches, wherever they have settlements, as I have before mentioned—and I was informed by an official who assisted in taking the census, that they can nearly all read and write. They have small houses simply built of round timber in the following manner : for a house 16 feet by 24 feet the sills are laid, six posts are hewn square, one for each corner and one in the middle lengthwise, grooves of two inches are cut in the posts in which plates are placed to hold the posts—then timbers are cut to the proper lengths and a two inch tenant made at either end to fit the groove in the posts; these timbers so prepared are slipped in between the posts in the grooves, one on top of the other, until the spaces are filled up to the plates, which are from eight to ten feet above the sills—thus forming the sides and ends of the building; the cracks and openings are all plastered over on the inside and outside and then whitewashed. Some of their buildings are only 16 feet square in which case only four posts are required.

The roof is made of poles laid close together in rafter form and filled out with clay, mortar and prairie grass puddled into the clay at one end, the butts of the grass covering the clay—this makes a tight and substantial roof—buildings thus constructed afford a warm house, and I would recommend settlers with limited means to adopt this plan for their houses, where the timber is so small that they cannot make them in the old Canadian style.

The reader might wonder why the Half-breeds rose in rebellion a few years ago, if they are civilized and satisfied. They thought that our Government should first consult them and give them a certain right to the lands they then occupied, and also lands for their children. An arrangement has now been come to between these people and the Government which gives to every man, woman and child living at that time, one hundred and forty acres of land; with this they are now satisfied, and they seem to be well pleased with the action of the Government.

INDIANS.

ARE THERE MANY INDIANS, AND ARE THEY PEACEABLY INCLINED ?

This is another question frequently put to me, and I can say in answer thereto, that as far as I could ascertain, they are both quiet and inoffensive and well satisfied with the Government from which they receive an annuity—three dollars to every soul annually—besides which they have hunting grounds for themselves far back in the North-West. If the agreement, as above, is carried out faithfully by our Government, and I have no doubt it will be, there will be no trouble from the Indians. The British Government has never yet had trouble with the Indians in Canada. The Indians who once enter into a treaty will keep it to the letter, but when a promise to them is broken, they are not only dissatisfied but will assuredly seek revenge. This, I am told, is what led to the trouble between the American Indians and the residents of some of the Western States, and was the cause of the dreadful massacre of the settlers, in Minnesota a few years ago.

The United States Government had made a treaty with the Indians, promising them a certain amount of money, out of part of which they were defrauded by the officials appointed to distribute the sums granted to them. I was told by an agent of the Hudson's Bay Company, that some of these American Indians, of the Sioux Tribe, have fled to the North-West of Canada, and that the Company frequently employs them to work at their trading posts, and that they are good workers and respect our Government very much. Our Canadian Indians are of the Chippewa Tribe, but are not very well well pleased that so many of the " Sioux " come in from the other side.

FROSTS, AND ADAPTATION OF CLIMATE TO AGRICULTURE.

I agree fully with the following remarks made by Mr. Spence in his pamphlet " Manitoba and the North-West of the Dominion."

"The liability to disastrous frosts in the season of growth, and which so
" intimately concerns the interests of husbandry, is not any worse in Manitoba
" than in many parts of Ontario. In the former province the spring of 1869
" was an exceptionally late one, and in May several light frosts were expe-
" rienced, but which did no serious damage to the crops; in fact the injury was
" scarcely noticeable; this may be accounted for from the following rea-
" sons :—1. The dryness of the atmosphere (which is a peculiarity of this re-
" gion) allows a much lower range of temperature, without injury to vegeta-
" tion, than in moister climates, and in addition to the heat, gives greater
" vigour to the plants, which grow rapidly but with firm texture, and are con-
" sequently able to resist severe cold on account of their excessive vitality, the
" same as a person who has partaken heartily of strong diet, is better able to
" resist the cold of winter. 2. The sudden change of temperature, which is
" often the case in this region,—one extreme following another in rapid succes-
" sion—is less deleterious to vigorous plants, than a gradual lowering of tem-
" perature. The earth and plants still retain the heat previously absorbed,
" and are thus enabled to bear an atmosphere at 20° much better than at 35°
" after latent heat has been given off. The soil of the prairie is generally dry—
" and is rapidly warmed by the rays of the sun in the spring. 3. The benefits
" arising from the dryness of the air are accounted for from the fact, that
" moisture conveyed in the air has a tendency to soften the delicate covering
" of the plants, and thus render them more sensitive to cold. 4. The heat-
" retaining character of the soil. For these and several other reasons that
" might be mentioned, the climate of Manitoba is less subject to killing frosts,
" than might at first be supposed to bo the case on account of its high lati-
" tude."

I was informed by Mr. Deputy Sheriff Nesbitt, of Winnipeg, that in the year
1870 the first fall frost of any consequence occurred on the 2nd of October, in the
year 1871, on the 15th of October, and last year in the latter part of
October, which shows that during the growing season, frosts are not likely to
do damage to the crops. With regard to spring frosts, Mr. Taylor, an aged
gentleman now upwards of eighty, and resident in that country about fifty-

yéars, informed me that he scarcely ever knew vegetables to suffer from frosts after they have once started in the spring.

The season opens, so I was informed by Messrs. McKenzie and Taylor, for spring ploughing from about the 20th of April to the 1st of May, after which they have very few frosts and cold is very moderate, as the seasons change rapidly from winter to summer—winter generally lasts five months, say from the middle of November to the middle of April. In the year 1871 snow fell very early, on the 12th November, but as a rule there is very little snow before Christmas. When I arrived there, 17th November, last fall, there was no snow. On the 1st of December there was a slight fall of snow, about an inch in depth.

Although the weather was very cold when I was in the Province, yet the air being clear and dry, the cold is not felt as much as it would be in Ontario, where the air is more moist. On the 23th and 29th November last year, the thermometer stood at 25° to 30° below zero. I was out riding in an open carriage both days, travelling from twelve to sixteen miles without making stoppages, and it did not appear colder to me than it does in Ontario when the thermometer is only from 5° to 10° below zero. During the days above mentioned I saw at several places as I was proceeding along, herds of cattle pasturing on the open prairies without shelter.

STOCK RAISING AND WOOL GROWING.

From experience of many years it is shown that Manitoba and the North West are good lands for stock raising, as the grass of the prairies is very nutritious, and the supply for many years will be inexhaustible. Although the weather is cold, the snow, as I said before, generally comes late—yet, notwithstanding, I would consider it more profitable to cut the grass for the winter season and have the cattle and stock sheltered, than to have them run at large as is the case in the States further South, where there is scarcely any snow, but where they have damp cold winds. It would not cost much to cut the grass with mowers, and then to stack it in ridges or rows as I have seen it at the Hudson's Bay Company's Posts and on several of the stock-raising farms. These stacks so made, form a shelter around the stable yards.

I think that wool growing would be the most profitable, as the climate is more suitable than in a warmer and damper air. The natives who have tried the experiment say that sheep do well, and no disease is known amongst the flocks. Wool is easily exported, and would command nearly the same price there as it does here and in the adjoining States, where land is dear, and where there is no hay but what is raised on the cultivated farm lands.

Another great advantage, favorable to the raising of cattle and sheep, is the enormous yield of turnips, carrots, and mangolds, in Manitoba, mentioned by me in the earlier pages of this report.

FRUIT CULTURE.

The culture of fruit, especially apples, has been entirely neglected in Manitoba hitherto; in fact there has never been a practical test made to really know whether fruit trees will flourish or not. This is owing, probably, to there being such abundance of wild fruit, and also to the difficulty of getting young trees for planting. The natives are entirely unacquainted with the culture of fruit t'ees, as they have been bred and b, rn without seeing any such under cultivation. When we find so great an abundance of wild fruit in the forests, I cannot but believe that many kinds of apples would do well in Manitoba, particularly along the edge of the timber lands. In the State of Minnesota, where the extreme snow storms prevail, and where it is fully as cold, they have very fine fruit. I saw young apple trees of two years' growth, raised from the seed by Mr. McKenzie, at Rat Creek, and they looked hearty and of a large size for a two years old growth. I would avise all settlers, once established, to plant apple seeds ; the expense would be only trifling, and trees grown from seed will will always be better adapted to the climate. After they have grown and have been transplanted about two years, then they should be top grafted with the hardy varieties suitable for cold climates, such as the Snow-apple (Fameuse) the Rambo, Northern Spy, Spitzenberg, Talman's, Sweeting, &c. I see no reason why apple trees should not thrive there, as it is not the degree of the cold that kills the trees, but the open and warm weather in the winter, thawing the earth and starting the sap ; afterwards freezing hard again to their injury. This is not a common occurrence in Manitoba.

The wild fruit in Manitoba consists of the wild plum, grapes, strawberries, currants, red and black raspberries, cherries, blueberries, wortleberries, high bush cranberries, &c., so that the emigrant need not suffer for the want of good fruit in abundance.

THE BEST TIME FOR THE SETTLER TO COME.

The settler should, if possible, be on his land by the 1st of June, when he would be in time to plant a patch of potatoes which will grow in an ordinary season when ploughed under the prairie sod. The ploughing for the next Spring's crop should be done in June or July, when the sap is in the roots of the grass ; being turned over at this season of the year it will dry up and the sod will rot, so that the ground will be in proper order for receiving and growing crops in the following Spring.

WHAT CAPITAL IS NECESSARY WITH WHICH TO COMMENCE.

This is a question frequently asked—the answer depends entirely upon surrounding circumstances. A young man without family, willing to work and save, would secure himself a home in a few years, provided he had only ten dollars to purchase a homestead claim. Work is to be had at high wages, and he could work for other parties part of the time, and then hire help again in turn to assist in putting up a small homestead house. After that he could plough and fence in a few acres for a crop in the following Spring. The next year he could earn enough to buy a yoke of oxen and other cattle, and thus, in a short time, he might become, comparatively, an independent farmer. A settler with a family ought to have provisions for one year (or the wherewithal to procure them).

Such a one, desiring to start comfortably should have the following articles, or the means to purchase them, viz :

One yoke of oxen	$120 00
One waggon	80 00
Plough and harrow	25 00
Chains, axes, shovels, &c	30 00
Stoves, beds, &c	60 00
House and stable, say	150 00
Total	$165 00

A person having $800 or $1,000 can, if he wishes to carry on farming on a large scale, purchase another quarter section in addition to his free grant, when he will have a farm of three hundred and twenty acres of land for cultivation, and in addition can cut all the hay he wants in the marshes, if he thinks it desirable.

DOMINION LANDS ACT.

The following is a summary of the Dominion Lands Act :

An Act was passed last Session (35 Vic., cap. 23) amending and consolidating the laws and Orders in Council respecting the public lands of the Dominion.

The administration and management is to be effected through a Branch of the Department of the Secretary of State of Canada, known as " *the Dominion Lands Office.*"

The surveys divide the lands into quadrilateral townships, containing 36 sections of one mile square in each, together with road allowances of one chain and fifty links in width, between all townships and sections.

Each section of 640 acres is divided into half sections of 320 acres, quarter sections of 160 acres, and half quarter sections of 80 acres. All townships and lots are rectangular. To facilitate the descriptions for Letters Patent of less than a half quarter section, the quarter sections composing every section in accordance with the boundaries of the same, as painted or placed in the original survey, shall be supposed to be divided into quarter quarter sections, or 40 acres. The area of any legal subdivision in Letters Patent shall be held to be more or less, and shall, in each case, be represented by the exact quantity as given to such subdivision in the original survey ; provided that nothing in the Act shall be construed to prevent the lands upon the Red and Assiniboine Rivers, surrendered by the Indians to the late Earl of Selkirk, from being laid out in such manner as may be necessary in order to carry out the clause of the Act to prevent fractional sections or lands bordering on any rivers, lake, or other water course or public road from being divided ; or such lands from being laid out in lots of any certain frontage and depth, in such manner as may appear desirable ; or to prevent the subdivision of sections or other legal subdivisions into wood lots ; or from describing the said lands upon the Red

4

52

and Assiniboine Rivers, or such subdivisions of wood lots, for patent, by numbers according to a plan of record, or by metes and bounds, or by both, as may seem expedient.

Unappropriated Dominion lands may at present be purchased at the rate of $1.00 per acre ; but no purchase of more than a section, or 640 acres, shall be made by the same person. Payments of purchase to be made in cash. The Secretary of State may, however, from time to time, reserve tracts of land, as he may deem expedient, for Town or Village plots, such lots to be sold either by private sale, and for such price as he may see fit, or at public auction. The Governor in Council may set apart lands for other public purposes, such as sites of market places, gaols, court-houses, places of public worship, burying grounds, schools, benevolent institutions, squares, and for other like public purposes.

Free grants of quarter sections, 160 acres, are made to any person who is the head of a family, or to any person not the head of a family who has attained the age of 21 years, on condition of three years' settlement, from the time of entering upon possession, provided the limitation of quantity shall not prevent the granting of a wood lot to the same person. When two or more persons have settled on and seek to obtain a title to the same land, the homestead right shall be in him who made the first settlement. If both have made improvements, a division of the land may be ordered in such manner as may preserve to the said parties their several improvements.

Questions as to the homestead right arising between different settlers shall be investigated by the Local Agent of the division in which the land is situated, whose report shall be referred to the Secretary of state for decision.

Every person claiming a homestead right from actual settlement must file his application for such claim with the Local Agent within 30 days after the date of such settlement, if in surveyed lands ; if in unsurveyed lands, within three months after such land shall have been surveyed.

No patent will be granted for land till the expiration of three years from the time of entering into possession of it.

When both parents die, without having devised the land, and leave a child or children under age, it shall be lawful for the executors (if any) of the last surviving parent, or the guardian of such child or children, with the approval of a Judge of a Superior Court of the Province or Territory in which the lands lie, to sell the lands for the benefit of the infant or infants, but for no other purpose ; and the purchaser in such a case shall acquire the homestead right by such purchase; and on carrying out the unperformed conditions of such right, shall receive a patent for the land upon payment of the office fees.

The title to lands shall remain in the Crown until the issue of the patent therefor, and such lands shall not be liable to be taken in execution before the issue of the patent.

If a settler voluntarily relinquishes his claim, or has been absent from the land entered by him for more than six months in any one year, then the right to such land shall be forfeited.

A patent may be obtained by any person before three years, on payment of price at the date of entry, and making proof of settlement and cultivation for not less than than 12 months from date of entry.

All assignments and transfers of homestead rights before the issue of the patent shall be null and void, but shall be deemed evidence of abandonment of the right.

These provisions apply only to homesteads and not to lands set apart as timber lands, or to those on which coal or minerals, at the time of entry, are known to exist.

GRAZING LANDS.

Unoccupied Dominion lands may be leased to neighboring settlers for grazing purposes; but such lease shall contain a condition making such land, liable for settlement or for sale at any time during the term of such lease without compensation, save by a proportionate deduction of rent, and a further condition by which, on a notice of six months, the Secretary of State may cancel the lease at any time during the term.

Unoccupied Dominion lands will be leased to neighboring settlers for the purpose of cutting hay thereon, but not to the hinderance of the sale and settlement thereof.

MINING LANDS.

As respects mining lands, no reservations of gold, silver, iron, copper or other mines or minerals will be inserted in any patent from the Crown, granting any portion of the Dominion lands. Any person may explore for mines or minerals on any of the Dominion public lands, surveyed or unsurveyed, and, subject to certain provisions, may purchase the same. As respects coal lands, they cannot be taken for homesteads.

TIMBER LANDS.

Provisions are made in the Act for disposing of the timber lands so as to benefit the greatest possible number of settlers, and to prevent any petty monopoly. In the subdivision of townships, consisting partly of prairie and partly of timber land, such of the sections as contain islands, belts, or other tracts of timber shall be subdivided into such number of wood lots, of not less than ten and not more than twenty acres in each lot, as will afford one such wood lot to each quarter section prairie farm in such township.

The Local Agent, as settlers apply for homestead rights in a township, shall apportion to each quarter section one of the adjacent wood lots, which shall be a free gift in connection with such homestead and in addition thereto.

Any homestead claimant who, previous to the issue of the patent, shall sell any of the timber on his claim, or on the wood lot appertaining to his claim, to saw-mill proprietors or to any other settlers for their own private use, shall be guilty of a trespass and may be prosecuted therefor, and shall forfeit his claim absolutely.

The word *timber* includes all lumber, and all products of timber, including firewood or bark.

The right of cutting timber shall be put up at a bonus per square mile, varying according to the situation and value of the limit, and sold to the highest bidder by competition, either by tender or by public auction.

The purchaser shall receive a lease for 21 years, granting the right of cutting timber on the land, with the following conditions: To erect a saw mill or mills in connection with such limit or lease, of a capacity to cut at the rate of 1,000 feet broad measure in 24 hours, for every two and a half square miles of limits in the lease, or to establish such other manufactory of wooden goods, the equivalent of such mill or mills, and the lessee to work the limit within two years from the date thereof, and during each succeeding year of the term ;

To take from every tree he cuts down all the timber fit for use, and manufacture the same into sawn lumber or some other saleable product;

To prevent all unnecessary destruction of growing timber on the part of his men, and to prevent the origin and spread of fires ;

To make monthly returns to Government of the quantities sold or disposed of—of all sawn lumber, timber, cordwood, bark, &c., and the price and value thereof ;

To pay, in addition to the bonus, an annual ground rent of $2,00 per square mile, and further, a royalty of 5 per cent. on his monthly account ;

To keep correct books, and submit the same for the inspection of the collector of dues whenever required.

The lease shall be subject to forfeiture for infraction of any of the conditions to which it is subject, or for any fraudulent return.

The lessee who faithfully carries out these conditions shall have the refusal of the same limits, if not required for settlement, for a further term not exceeding 21 years, on payment of the same amount of bonus per square mile as was paid originally, and on such lessee agreeing to such conditions, and to pay such other rates as may be determined on for such second term.

The standard measure used in the surveys of the Dominion is the English measure of length.

Dues to the Crown are to bear interest, and to be a lien on timber cut on limits. Such timber may be seized and sold in payment.

Any person cutting timber without authority on any Dominion lands, shall, in addition to the loss of his labour and disbursements, forfeit a sum not exceeding $3 for each tree he is proved to have cut down. Timber seized, as forfeited, shall be deemed to be condemned, in default of owner claiming it within one month.

FORM OF APPLICATION FOR A HOMESTEAD RIGHT.

I,   of   do hereby apply to be entered, under the provisions of the *Act respecting the Public Lands of the Dominion* for quarter quarter sections numbers   and   forming part of section number .   of the Township of   containing   acres, for the purpose of securing a homestead right in respect thereof.

AFFIDAVIT IN SUPPORT OF CLAIM FOR HOMESTEAD RIGHT,

I, A. B., do solemnly swear (or affirm, as the case may be), that I am over 21 years of age, and that my application for leave to be entered for lands, with a view of securing a homestead right therein, is made for my exclusive use and benefit, and that the entry is made for the purpose of actual settlement. So help me God.

INDEX.

——o——

www.ingramcontent.com/pod-product-compliance
Lightning Source LLC
Chambersburg PA
CBHW031757090426
42739CB00008B/1052